TIME IS NOT A RIVER

Michael Minassian

TRANSCENDENT ZERO PRESS
HOUSTON, TEXAS

Copyright © 2020, Michael Minassian.

PUBLISHED BY TRANSCENDENT ZERO PRESS
www.transcendentzeropress.org

All rights reserved. No part or parts of this book may be reproduced in any format whether electronic or in print except as brief portions used in reviews, without the expressed written consent of Transcendent Zero Press, or of the author Michael Minassian.

ISBN-13: 978-1-946460-04-2
Library of Congress Control Number: 9781946460042

Printed in the United States of America

Transcendent Zero Press
16429 El Camino Real Apt. #7
Houston, TX 77062

Cover artwork: "Incomplete", Christine Karapetian
Cover Design: Glynn Monroe Irby

FIRST EDITION

TIME IS NOT A RIVER

Michael Minassian

Acknowledgements

"Black & White Cows." *Third Wednesday*. Spring 2015
"Blue Bodies Litter the Beach." *Iodine Poetry Journal*. 2011.
"The British Museum." *Exit 7*. 2014.
"Calligraphy." *The Arboriculturist* (Chapbook). 2010.
"The Cartographer." *San Pedro Review*, 2017.
"The Children Send Postcards." *4th and Sycamore*, 2016.
"Collage." *The Comstock Review*. 2014.
"Counting Words." *Poetry Quarterly*, 2016.
"The Cut Above the Heart." *Main St. Rag*, 2017.
"Crazy Jane Talks to Me." *Savannah Literary Journal*, 1998.
"Death of the Postcard." *New Ulster,* 2017.
"Early One Morning." *The Lake.* March 2016.
"Eyes on Fire" *Diverse Voices Quarterly*, 2010.
"Ficus Benghalensis" Dos Passos Review 2007
"Gwen's Lament." *The Broken Plate*, 2014.
"The House is Full," *4th and Sycamore*, 2016.
"An Icicle." *The Galway Review.* 2015.
"I Know You are Not a Scientist." Comstock Review, 2017.
"Like Black Rocks." *The Galway Review.* 2016.
"Let's Burn the Bed" *3rd Wednesday.* 2009.
"Like Black Rocks." *The Galway Review.* 2015.
"Mermaid Skeleton" *The Maine Review*, 2018.
"Nano Heartbreaks" *Iodine Poetry Journal*, 2014.
"Needle and Ink; Feathers and Wax." *Curbside Review*. 2002.
"On the Maryland Coast." *Verse-Virtual*. March, 2016.
"The Party." *The Comstock Review*. Spring/Summer 2014: 82.
"Poetry Origami." *4th & Sycamore*. Publication Pending, 2016.
"Postcard from Key West." *Main Street Rag*. Spring 2012: 62-63.
"Postcard from the Side of the Road." Meadow, 2015.
"Postcard on Reverse" *The Meadow*, Summer 2014: 84.
"Postcard from Russia." *The Meadow.* Summer 2013.
"The Restaurant of Books." *Nebo*, Fall 2011.
"The Rosenbergs Come Out to Play." Poet Lore, 2018.
"The Seed of Gold." *Poet Lore.* 2006.
"Sheep on the Moon." *Harbinger Asylum*, 2018.
"The Short Story." *The Meadow,* 2013.
"Superman Lived Next Door." *Kakalak* 2017.
"A Taste of Lavash." *White Pelican Review.* 2007.

"This Autumn Day." *Comstock Review*. 2016
"The Winter Day." *The Lake*. 2017.
"This is my Ghost Shirt." *Visions International*. #82, 2010.
"The Woodcutter's Axe." *Bitter Oleander:* 2006.

Table of Contents –

Part I - You Call This History

Eyes on Fire / 11
The Rosenbergs Come Out to Play / 12
Marie Antoinette in Vietnam / 15
Karl Marx in Heaven / 16
Taste of Lavash / 18
Ficus Benghalensis / 20
Gwen's Lament / 21
You Call This History / 22
History Follows You Home / 23
I Heard a River / 25
Sheep on the Moon / 26
Remember the Starving Armenians / 27
The Fallout Shelter / 29
Superman Lived Next Door / 31
I Know You Are Not a Scientist / 32
Crazy Jane Talks to Me / 33
The Woodcutter's Axe / 35
The Drowning / 36
You Are on the History Channel / 37
The Seed of Gold / 38

Part II – The Postcard Blues

The Postcard on Reverse / 45
Postcard from Key West / 46
Counting Words / 47
Nano Heartbreaks / 48
The Party / 49
Postcard from Russia / 50
An Icicle / 51
The Children Send Postcards / 52
Death of the Postcard / 53
Postcard from a Fiend / 54
Postcard Found on the Side of the Road / 55
The Postcard I Left Behind / 56
The Saint on My Lawn / 57

The British Museum / 58
The Knocking at the Gate / 59
Postcard from the Edge of the Lake / 60
On the Maryland Coast / 61
A Mermaid Skeleton is Found Off the Gulf Coast / 62
Blue Bodies Litter the Beach / 63

Part III – Let's Burn the Bed

Let's Burn the Bed / 67
She Never Said Goodbye / 69
Needle and Ink, Feathers and Wax / 70
To Tremble, Then Awake / 71
The Cut Above the Heart / 72
Pretending / 73
The Disappearance / 74
The Cartographer / 75
Confessions of a Sex Fiend / 76
I Always Cry at the Movies / 77
Raising Pigeons / 78
In the Back Yard / 79
Draw Me! / 80
Calligraphy / 81
This Autumn Day / 82
This Winter Day / 83

Part IV – Like Black Rocks

The Arboriculturist / 87
Like Black Rocks / 88
Black and White Cows in the Rain / 89
A Black and Red Ribbon / 90
I Loved Those Jersey Girls / 91
Forgotten Stops / 92
The Short Story / 93
My Friend Writes Poetry When She Can't Sleep / 94
Early One Morning / 95
Queen of the Wasps / 96
The Poet Barters for Words / 97
Collecting Jellyfish / 98
This is my Ghost Shirt / 99

Collage / 100
The House is Full / 101
The Restaurant of Books / 102

Part I – You Call This History

EYES ON FIRE

With what burning eyes
do I see the past

the black ash
that eats the edges
of the photographs,

the white ash
that covers my eyelids?

With what burning throat
do I recite the names
no one alive remembers,

names I have reduced to titles,
events, and relationships:

great-grandmother,
brother who drowned in Lake Van,
grandfather's first wife and son?

with what burning ears
do I hear the wind
traveling from the past;

the sound reaching my brain
with a series of sharp
cracks and scratches,

like old 78 rpm recordings;
the labels written in English
and Armenian –

one language bleeding
into the other,
as the record begins to spin

and I hear the music:

duduk, oud, my own voice?
THE ROSENBERGS COME OUT TO PLAY

I

The children wriggle
out the front door
of the apartment
and pause at the top
of the steps, talking quietly
and holding hands—hoping
the neighbors won't notice.
(Julius taller and thinner—
Ethel, wears glasses
too big for her face.)

Is this the zoo? they ask,
then laugh as they wait
to cross the street,
both of them speaking at once,
watching the elephants
march by on their way
from the Midtown Tunnel
to Madison Square Garden
to join the circus.

A few of the trainers
walk alongside
the lumbering animals,
silently linked trunk to tail.

(Overhead, planes
carrying bombs
crisscross the sky.)

II

Ethel stands on her cot
straining to reach
the window three feet
above her head.

She can barely see a patch of sky
and a cloud that looks like
a ragged piece of toast;
thick glass behind the bars
keeps the fresh air
outside her cell,
but she claims she smells
the river through the thick brick walls.

Somewhere in the men's block,
her husband's hunched
over a pad of paper,
writing letters to their two sons—
explaining that the name
of the prison came from
the Wappinger Indians,
who once owned
this place called Sint-Sinck—
another race exterminated
over sheets of paper
and parchment bearing
the names of dead chiefs.

III

Two years after the trial—
two years since the last time
they saw each other—

Ethel waits for Julius's turn.
She's heard through the grapevine
that the chair has a hard seat,
and the leather straps
are pulled too tight.

She's led in ten minutes
after his body is removed—
the air still thick with smoke
and the stench of burning.

He removed his glasses first,
just before the lights flickered,
and remembered
the march of elephants
outside the tenement door,

their smell mingling
with Ethel's peppermint breath
as she leaned
close to his cheek
and whispered in his ear
You go first.

Marie Antoinette In Vietnam

Marie Antoinette steps off the plane
wearing her diamond necklace,
complaining about the heat.

At the hotel, she takes off
her gown and wig,
tired of palace rebellions
and Robespierre,
she calls the staff
at the front desk comrade.

Interviewed on the radio
she denies the divine rights
of kings and queens,
condemning the use of napalm
and chemical weapons.

Years later she appears
wearing an *ao dai*
and white silk pants
baking cakes and practicing
English for the tourists.

Her specialty, an elaborate
cake made of flour and cream,
topped by a miniature
working guillotine,
and the words "Pardon me, sir,
I meant not to do it,"
written in pink frosting,
topped by a red star.

Karl Marx In Heaven

"The last capitalist we hang shall be the one who sold us the rope."
-   Karl Marx

He wanders around
looking for the means
of production;
no work being done
nothing produced.

Passing the sullen
saints and seraphim
he looks for signs
of proletarians, workers
and their chains.

The angels stick together
ignoring the mortals
who crowd around
bumping into each other
like sheep shorn of wool.

The recently dead mistake
him for one of the prophets
or Roman saints,
complaining about the lack
of leisure activities
asking directions to the ATM
and how to turn off
the constant Muzak:
harps and harpsichords—
speakers nesting
in every cloud.

He searches for libraries
and books, pen and paper,
years pass, centuries
dissolve one into another,
fading into the background
like white noise
or his beard that refuses to grow.

Eternity is too long,
he thinks to himself
muttering in German—
time moves or not at all—
the angels bickering
among themselves,
of gods, he has seen none.

The Taste of *Lavash*

My grandfather builds the fire first,
piling twigs and cut logs,
using last week's Armenian
newspaper as kindling –
the characters of the printed page
merging and melting
into another alphabet
of heat and flame.

Next, a square sheet of tin
is placed over the grate
of the backyard fireplace,
as my aunts carry out
bowls and water
to a table sitting under the trees -
a house built of sand and wind.

My grandmother wipes her forehead
leaving behind a trace of white flour,
like the names of the dead
she has whispered in my ear,
as she kneads and rolls
out pieces of dough,
then transfers each one
to a wooden paddle
I help carry to the fire.

Later, we smear fresh butter
on each section of round, flat bread
we roll up before eating;
the salt from our sweat
mingled with the flavor
of hot buttered *lavash*,
like a communion
for those left behind –
a thin, crisp palimpsest
of names and lives held in ash,
melting and merging

into images so old
they precede language:
just the pure flash of memory,
taste, and bread

Ficus Benghalensis

I like the quiet blue house
at the end of the block,
the one next to the tall banyan tree:

they say Jack Kerouac
lived there '57 to '58
and wrote the *Dharma Bums*
on one long continuous scroll

like some beat Bedouin
scribe burying sacred texts
inside pottery jars
in the back of caves -

sharing space with his mother,
typewriter and a bottle,
sometimes he felt
so cramped he slept

in the backyard
beneath the dangling roots
of the banyan tree

like a priest or goat herder
dreaming of America
in the long paragraph
of the past:

Orlando, the dead sea,
the hanging gardens of Babylon.

Gwen's Lament

He appeared out of the forest:
five thousand sharp blades of sunlight
piercing a canopy of treetops
like a torn veil across my eyes
burning, burning until only the torch
of his silhouette remained stark
against a world held as still
as the silent stones of my convent cell.

What matters my wordless cries
my waterless tears, my heartless love,
my husband's dry beard –
I touch my lips to his forehead,
beg forgiveness, yet my lover remains
here in the invisible world he alone discovered
which I could not imagine until he touched its shore.

You Call This History

I have seen the postcards
proclaiming history is dead,
then read the rings of fallen trees.

Birds compete with cancelled stamps,
aligning themselves in two straggling
rows, angel or devil, masked or disguised,

writing stories or washing poems
in the night sky while looking up
at children being born in secret.

Driving along Old Country Road
in a fast car, backwards, cows and corn
fields dance in the moonlight;

there is a waltz playing somewhere
from farm houses and an AM radio
tuned to the last half of the 20th century;

the handwriting on reverse resembles
a cursive not unlike a faded photograph;
in the corner, a face you call your own.

History Follows You Home

I was standing on the corner
in downtown San Antonio
across the street from the Alamo,
thinking about Santa Anna
and Felix the Cat
when a black guy with dreads
and a Spurs t-shirt said:
"Can you help me, I'm homeless."
But I was too stressed out
worrying about Mexican history
and an anthropomorphic cat
and maybe hung over
on too many *cervezas*,
so hurried away
feeling bad afterwards,
and the next time a panhandler
asked me for money,
I gave him all my change,
some jelly beans, and Santa Anna's
prosthetic wooden leg,
which just goes to show you
that history is not dead;
it follows you home
and when you wake up
the next morning, drools
on your pillow and follows
you around day after day
until even the neighbor
you still get along with
asks how long your guest
is going to stick around,
and you have no answer,
until one Saturday morning
Felix cartoons come on the TV,
and history slinks out the door
threatening to come back

so you shout out: "don't let
the door hit you on the ass
on your way out."

and smile when Felix takes
on the whole Mexican army
with his bag of tricks
and his own *mariachi* band
and Santa Anna, chewing nervously
on his moustache, retreats
all the way back to Mexico City
with both his legs still intact.

I Heard a River

I heard a river behind a closed door;
it told me a secret for which I had yearned
of the dead who slumber and wait for more.

History repeating whatever came before,
waiting for the past to return;
I heard a river behind a closed door.

Shaking off dust and bullets and gore,
bread and bones and all that was learned
of the dead who slumber and wait for more.

The wind blows up from the Mexican wars;
the ashes of the past escape from the urn;
I heard a river behind a closed door.

Borders shift, open, close, then bodies pour,
hunger and thirst in the desert burn;
the dead slumber and wait for more.

Santa Anna, Villa, Aztec kings all implore;
voices from below I can now discern.
I heard a river behind a closed door
of the dead who slumber and wait for more.

Sheep on the Moon

Just last night
I stood in the backyard,
wondering about the sheep
grazing on the mountains
of the moon, the ones
Neil Armstrong claimed
he had seen the time
his camera jammed –
no one believed him then,
but I think he knew
what he had seen:
a flock of muzzles
aimed at earth,
mathematical
equations as sharp
as the return home,
and life on earth
six times heavier
than walking on the moon.

REMEMBER THE STARVING ARMENIANS

In my mother's kitchen
food was weaponized
plates piled high with pilaf
tomatoes, chicken, and lamb.

Remember the starving Armenians,
my mother said.

History sat down at the table with us;
our lost family kept alive
half a century later
In Northern New Jersey,
Long Island, and the Bronx.

During the First Genocide
of the Twentieth Century,
America sent ships full
of food, nurses, and nuns
to the Mediterranean;
posters hung in town squares
and full-page ads appeared
in the New York Times:

Remember the starving Armenians

A million and a half dead,
another million scattered
around the world.

But I had to finish my dinner
no matter how full I felt
and if any scraps
remained on our plates
my mother stood
at the kitchen sink
and licked each one clean –

our kitchen at least
one place on earth
we ate for the empty places
we ate for the dead.

The Fallout Shelter

My father came into the house
night after night
caked with mud and sweat,
hiding from the neighbors
his secret plans for survival;
digging the foundation in the backyard,
hammering the frame,
placing each concrete block by hand
while we watched
from the kitchen window,
my sister, my mother, and I,
as the shelter grew like a fabulous
underground root.

Until the day he woke us just before dawn,
and we marched through the morning mist,
following like blind moles
after an all night binge of moonlight
to the carefully concealed entrance
behind the forsythia bushes
next to the ramshackle tool shed
he had painted dull civil defense yellow.

Finally, we emerged
into the suite of cell like rooms,
a bare Edison bulb dangling
from the white washed ceiling,
one room lined with shelves
filled not with the jars of food,
saltine tins, and jugs of water
we half expected, but instead
books of poetry and long lost novels,
Picasso prints and Rembrandt self-portraits,
my parent's wedding photo
and tiny handprints of my sister and me at birth
leaned up against my grandmother's
hand crocheted lace doily.

In the other room, in place of the radio
and toilet we surely needed to survive
99 years of radioactive fallout,
stood an odd assortment of mid-twentieth
century artifacts rescued from the attic
and an ancient manual Remington typewriter
to write wild manifestos from the past.

As my father showed us each
treasure and trophy, he began to cry,
great gigantic tears pooling
in the corner of his eyes,
then cascading down his cheeks
like a hieroglyph of runaway regrets
until my mother kissed his hand
and led him silently back above ground.

Later, the bomb shelter
became our playhouse,
even long into our teens –
a place to sneak down with our dates
and fumble in the dank darkness,
lighting candles and gawking
at my father's ruined imagination
like some subterranean tea party:
a place to savor scones and sonnets
and once every century perhaps
scent the perfumed night air.

Superman Lived Next Door

When I was just a kid,
Superman lived next door;
of course, he had lost
his super powers by then
and only wore his costume
and cape on the 4th of July.

Most times he sat around
the house drinking beer
working on his scrapbook;
sometimes at night,
you could catch the green
glow of Kryptonite he kept
in an empty aquarium
in his living room.

When I got drafted,
he let me hide out
in his Fortress of Solitude,
but I damn near froze to death;
later, he helped me get a job
on the local newspaper;
after work we'd listen
to the Kinks' song and laugh
*at the weakling with knobby
knees*, the one we all become
in the end, Kal-el said,
folding his Clark Kent
glasses and business suit:
"Who do you want to be today?"
he asked me before he finally
disappeared down in Florida
right before the last moon shot,
the one that never returned.

I Know You Are Not a Scientist

Dear Friend, the letter begins,
I am sorry to tell you
that the earth is indeed round,
no matter how many
two dimensional drawings
you produce. And, yes,
it is true that I had a lonely
childhood, and suffered
mightily, having not even
an imaginary friend,
though I found at an early age
that I could communicate
not only with animals
and birds, but also fish
and mammals of the sea;
there I am in the photograph
on page one of today's
newspaper, holding up a globe,
though slightly misshapen,
riding on the back
of a blue whale as it leaps
from the ocean to sing
the song made, as you know,
without vocal cords.

Hence, this letter;
if you cannot sing,
simply hum the tune
as it wanders
through your mind
like the sun revolving
around the earth,
and the planets
spinning like plates
in the circus of air.

Crazy Jane Talks to Me

Crazy Jane talks to me every night
in her low husky voice
she gives good phone sex -
electronic photon optic fiber head.

I'm writing a new Edgar Allan Poe story;
his heroines were always entombed,
never buried,
so they could walk again.

Crazy Jane visits me & pounds on the door -
I notice her panties around her ankle
like a thin bracelet of lace,
symbolic and glistening
with the dampness of her madness.

On the home shopping network
they are selling tape recorders and dope;
a man with hard gemlike eyes
and a crooked mustache appears
wearing a black suit and bow tie;
he faces the camera and speaks:

"Your name is Edgar Allan Poe;
You didn't die in Baltimore;
you are alive - your mouth is a road
others travel; your words are a map
of the future and streets of graveyards,
    I am sure."

The air is full of moths and butterflies;
Crazy Jane's brain is aflame,
her body feverish and wet;
the fan above the bed cuts
through the air like two stiff sets of wings.

Crazy Jane says: "I had a dream about you;
you were lying in a hospital bed;
tubes and things were coming out of your nose;
a pendulum, gleaming sharp and cold,
swung suspended over your body."

In the tale, the murderer says:
"The disease sharpened my senses;
observe how calmly I can tell you the whole story."

The Woodcutter's Axe

The wood cutter works alone
in the forest – even the birds
fall silent
at the clack-clack of his axe.

He shifts his weight
to his good knee
and pauses in mid-chop.

At the well, the girl
drinks from a cup
lowered into the water
twenty feet below

bringing it to her lips
she tastes blood, sawdust,
her father's saliva –
    the woodcutter's axe.

The Drowning

As I watched her take a bath
she sank down
until only her knees
and the top of her head
showed above the surface

"Call me, Ophelia," she said.

"Call me, Ishmael," I replied
unscrewing my wooden leg.

You know how it ends:
all drowned

shipwrecked
and poisoned

whale bones
on the Danish shore

dead princes
and a suicide note

the ghost of a chance.

You Are on The History Channel

You've got your feet
propped up on the coffee table
in front of the couch
watching late night TV
startled to see yourself
as a guest, talking about
the stock market, box office
receipts, and your biography
on the History Channel,
the one that has you
walking with Jesus and Lao Tzu
through the Lincoln Tunnel,
emerging from the past
into the future.

The documentary's narrator
speaking in a dolorous voice,
suddenly breaks into song,
the same one that was sung
at your cremation
a thousand years ago
when you were still young.

You, who could never
wrap your mind around
the idea of reincarnation,
can now remember your other
lives, yes, even the ant
and the elephant.

And now you wonder
what is it that is coming next.

The Seed of Gold

I.

Milan, Italy - 1492

Leonardo stares at the object
on the desk in front of him:
clearly, it is a cell phone,
but he has no name for it:

tinkering with his alchemist's tools,
he has teleported this object
from the future back in time to Milan;

intending to transmute
gold from base metals,
he has instead transversed
the space/time continuum.

*   *   *

Leonardo picks up the cell phone
and places it on a scale:
counterbalancing the tray with lead,
he removes the object from the scale
and measures it with an ivory ruler
carved from an elephant tusk -

he flips open the phone
and examines the hinge:
perhaps he has discovered
a design
for his flying machine?

For the next week
he pushes buttons,
numbers, and other symbols
on the keypad

in random sequences,
finding lists, more numbers
in odd patterns, names, paintings,
(he has no word for photograph)
ring tones, games, calendars,
databases, and a calculator,
which he develops into a 15th century
model for a device
that proves the earth
revolves around the sun.

One day Leonardo is startled awake
when the phone rings,
and he instinctively flips it open:

a disembodied voice speaks
through some sorcery or scientific genius,
Leonardo is no longer sure
if there is a difference between the two.

Leonardo holds the phone at arm's length
and screams at it:

"Why don't you speak Italian?"

II

The United States - 2006

Mikial stares at the notebook
on the coffee table -
it has materialized suddenly
like a wounded bird:

a leather-bound book
full of drawings, diagrams,
mathematical equations;
page after page
written in an elegant archaic handwriting
he recognizes as Italian.

He picks up the notebook
but cannot use it to make a call,
plan his day, check his e-mail;
he misses his cell phone
and decides to call the number:

the ringing sounds odd
as if it were underwater
in a tunnel…

After a long delay
a connection is made -
an angry voice
on the other end of the line
yells at him in Italian:

"Perchè non parlate italiano?"

* * *

Mikial studies the notebook for the next week:
although he can't read Italian,
he discovers Leonardo used mirror writing
starting at the right side of the page
and moving to the left,

but Mikial never thinks to hold
the notebook up to the mirror,
so does not realize he is holding
the missing notebook
of Leonardo da Vinci.

III.

**Leonardo's Quarters at the Palace
of Duke Ludovico**

Leonardo can no longer coax
the phone to perform
its science or sorcery,
he doesn't care which.

Growing bored with the object,
he places it into a box
next to a letter to a Polish prodigy
named Copernicus
and a working model of a submarine.

He opens a new notebook
and scribbles an equation,
tears it up, and decides
to abandon science for art:
his alchemist's tools, lead
and gold melted down
to pigment, ink, and paint.

Part II – The Postcard Blues

The Postcard on Reverse

I am writing to you
from somewhere in history,
illogical though that may seem.

Time, you see, is not just a river;
it's a group of islands
& the wooden skeleton

of a wrecked steamboat;
while this place itself took a builder's pen
& one hundred years to complete,

plus twelve dead workers, happy
in their sacrifice, eating out
of lunch pails & sarcophagi.

The cathedral pictured on the reverse
is a drawing made too late
even for photography;

notice the stained-glass windows
when lit by the sun
like a row of teeth, sharpened.

Postcard from Key West

I've been thinking about you
the whole damn ride
down from Miami on US 1
in the long tunnel of fog
and rain, through the Upper
and Lower Keys and over
the seven-thousand-mile bridge
past the seven thousand white cranes
that seemed to shadow my car
and skirt between the palm trees,
mangroves, and the flat green water
that merges the Gulf of Mexico
and the Atlantic Ocean,
as if it were really two separate bodies
of water that should know
their own boundaries;
like you saying you wanted your own space:
so, tell me, how do you "own" space.

I finally got down to this hotel,
where the only room left had a busted a/c
and last night I heard about a dozen
roosters three hours before dawn
and now I'm sitting in a Cuban café
drinking *café con leche*
and thinking about calling you,
but instead I ask for the check
then head for the beach
where I hope the mosquitoes
won't find me and I can watch the waves
roll in and roll out, and I suddenly realize
that love is like the Overseas Highway:
sometimes the road doesn't go on anymore –
you reach the end of the continent
and the only thing in front of you is the blank sea
and behind the same plunging pavement
pointing back in the opposite direction

while a drunken hurricane lurks by the side of the road.

Counting Words

Driving past the Alamo
yesterday, you counted
the people in the square
huddled around the entrance.

The mission shone white
in the glare of the sun,
and I counted the bullet
holes in the façade,
black spots against
the reflected stone:
wounds that would not heal.

Later that night,
you counted the stars
in the night sky
while we searched
for the right words
to say goodbye;
I counted heartbeats,
first yours, then mine.

In the distance, a train
whistle blew, counting
the miles between
words and the wind
and then you were gone.

Nano Heartbreaks

At first, your postcard made no sense:
especially the references to Fellini
films and Felix the Cat
immediately following
the salutation and obligatory
concerns for my family's health.

Not until the 3rd reading
did I understand the comments
about monuments and car crashes,
lost civilizations and washing machines,
but by then it was too late.

Buried behind the words,
between each letter of the alphabet,
tiny razor blades worked their way
under my skin, nano heartbreaks
staining the photo on reverse
with streaks of blood,
like shooting stars on the last
night before the new moon.

The Party

    I have brewed a perfume made of honey
to serve at your party
in place of citrus juice and green melons;
I have brought dancing sweet cakes
made of bee wings and the breath of the sun.

    In all the streets of the city
I have searched for you above
& below ground; looked on rooftops,
under lawn mowers, and in bakeries;
where have you gone?
the guests wait, crowding the sidewalks;
the line stretches for forty blocks;
like a parade where everyone is told not to move,
they fall asleep where they stand,
asphalt for pillows, letters arrived in place of dreams
made of bee wings and the breath of the sun.

    Your voice arises to meet mine,
& I try to spell out your name
with my tongue,
repeating after you pronounce
each word, as if we shared
the same accent, silk & flame,
like a whisper heard across the water
made of bee wings and the breath of the sun.

Postcard from Russia

Above us the clouds stack up
like suitcases & steamer trunks

piled up in the murderer's apartment
waiting for the delayed journey

to the cemetery or perhaps
a long ride on the train East;

time enough to write a short novel
or to crack the case

before the unnamed protagonist,
speaking faster than a lighted match,

swallows whole sentences,
paragraphs disappearing like smoke,

words spilling onto the front of his shirt
then dropping like ash onto the floor:

    Along the tree-lined avenue
the widows stand still, mute statues

among the upturned branches,
burdened by the guilt of lost sons & husbands;

then march like blackbirds
brushing their wings against the trees

as rain falls and the sky bends
revealing teeth & the space between words.

An Icicle

I could have chosen a postcard
to send to you with scenes
from the beach, perhaps one
of those jokey ones with an alligator
pulling down the bikini bottom
of a pretty girl with red lips and purple hair,
or maybe a drawing of a pink elephant
having a fruity drink at some tiki bar.

But instead I chose this card:
ice covered trees and a pitiless blue sky
to remind me that I am standing
ankle deep in discarded words
and frozen phrases, the letters I wanted
to write, now down to a single
text message, a hash tag
of cold winter wings:
an icicle hanging from my lips.

The Children Send Postcards

The children send postcards
to their parents, missing
since birth, lost in a parking
lot behind the empty hospital,

the one that used to be a church
and before that the town jail,
built on the ruins of a newspaper
office that once published

the names of unwed mothers
and the anonymous fathers
buried on boot hill, the old
wooden crosses leaning into each

other as if they would hear
what the other confessed –
no one goes up there anymore,
not even to deliver the mail.

Death of the Postcard

On a creased rectangle
of thin cardboard
words appear indecipherable,
smeared and running
from rain or a teardrop;

what matters is the method –
the elegant sprawl of handwriting,
the plaintive tone
of the wounded lover,
the razor slash of goodbye,
the guilty rant of the culpable
no matter how innocent –

the quaint communiqué
before the advent of the acronym,
twitter, and text shorthand:

the slight elevation
of the aching heart
a forgotten eyelash
the lover's sigh:

what does open
communication
really mean?

Postcard from a Fiend

I'm writing to you as a friend;
without the "r" that would be a fiend
since I sensed the card you sent me
was really a kiss off although you said
you wished that I was there
to record my own images & memories,
but I noticed that you never once
mentioned yourself except as a detached
observer or said that you missed me,
& even though all I could think about
when you were gone was your mouth
with the silken tongue & lips of fire,
it seems you were thinking about the biscuits
you ate that morning & how they stuck
to the roof of your mouth,
as if that were the taste of love.

Postcard Found on The Side of The Road

Tire tracks and insect guts
darken the photo on reverse

of a roadhouse painted red –
a neon guitar and bottle of beer

on the roof, and on the backside
in the space for an address:

two words: *you bastard*
then a street and city name

and the only message, somewhat
smeared by tears or whiskey:

You know who this is....

The Postcard I Left Behind

By the time you read this,
it will be too late to say I'm sorry;

I'll leave the clichés to the writers
of checklists and sculptors of trees;

for the truth, I will substitute
trail mix and wildflowers:

toadflax and forget-me-nots;
for lies, I will swallow bird calls

unanswered, carrying only my backpack
and copies of the sonnets you left behind.

On the path ahead, I see the bear scat
and crushed weeds, the paw prints;

eaten by a bear, or bearing to be eaten,
what's the opposite of zero?

the sharp teeth, the claws;
I imagined an allegory, not a feast.

The Saint on My Lawn

The statue of a saint on my lawn
bends his head every dawn,
begging forgiveness and struggling to speak,
as blood red tears, slashes of paint, leak
from the blank holes drilled for eyes,
a plaster reminder of his own demise.

Sainthood, he discovered, no guarantee
to shed both blindness and catastrophe;
leaving behind the burden of sainthood
like a tree shedding leaf, bark, and wood,
he claims to not deserve praise or pain;
the very reason, I suspect, he remains.

My own duty, to cut his hair, *un milagro,*
which un-bid and unwanted continues to grow.

The British Museum

In the British Museum, nude statues
from ancient Greece & Rome
line the corridors & galleries;
the male figures all missing
a penis, leaving only a broken
off jagged stump in its place,
just below the walnut shaped scrotum
covered with a fine white marble dust.

Perhaps it was the Victorians,
my companion says, or a marauding
band of bowdlerizers brandishing
umbrellas, dictionaries, and chisels;
but I prefer to think the culprits
are the female statues, goddesses
& slaves alike, lacking limbs, a nose,
or a single breast, who have chopped off
each phallus & saved the pieces for a nightly ritual:

You can hear them long after closing hours
when the weight of centuries gives way
to the darkness settling over sleep,
armless and shining in the moonlight
giggling together or giving out a low soft moan.

The Knocking at The Gate

This day seems like any other,
watching the hummingbirds
through the kitchen window;
hard work, I imagine,
flapping wings so fast,
they seem to stand mid-air,
hunting for food, spiders and insects,
and the occasional sweet snack.

They hover and dart from plant
to plant, flower to flower,
while I fill my coffee cup
a second time, adding sugar
and cream, dreaming
of gardens on earth
and angels beating
their wings, descending
to deliver a message.

No wonder the women
look so frightened
in the old paintings—
nothing good ever came
from a knock on the door
in the middle of the night,
or the sound of rushing
wings, hovering just above
your bed, time standing
as still as an unwanted caress.

Postcard from The Edge of The Lake

Welcome to the edge of the lake:
let me introduce the promises
you'll make and the ones you'll break;
like you said, it's all hit and miss.

What we don't talk about is not the past,
it's the future, an autobiography
you write backwards; the last
misunderstanding: love's atrophy.

Curled up inside the book case,
you waited for angels, heard the rush
of wings, but I recognized the distaste
in the marginalia, the words you crushed.

Water has its own grammar,
a stark separation of depth and light,
the blow comes as quick as a hammer;
let the sound carry itself away in flight.

On the Maryland Coast

In an old notebook, I found a few lines
I had written down the night we met,
just that one time, when I stayed
in your house on the Maryland coast,
each of us with someone else,
the night you & I talked about writing,
reading our latest poems aloud
before finishing the last bottle of wine:
you had a funny way of saying my name
tilting your head every time you looked my way;
you were so intense, your face a map
not too different from my own story.

Later, while the moon danced
on the ocean's dark secret waves,
I lay awake long into the night
thinking of you in the upstairs bedroom
hunkered over your journal
writing this poem or perhaps
holding the other half of a branch
whose leaves scattered long ago.

A Mermaid Skeleton Is Found Off the Gulf Coast

Lured by the postcard you sent me
about the mermaid skeleton
found off the Gulf Coast,
I arrive in Florida:
from the tops of lifeguard stations
flags fly: blue, green, yellow,
red, black, & purple;
a color for every danger.

On the beach in Naples, waves roll in
spilling sand, shells, & fragments of bones;
dark skinned dolphins, sleek & graceful
arrive in clusters under the pier;
they break the surface then dive again,
proposing marriage with the voices of angels
in a strange language that sounds like Norwegian
to women lining the rails.

That night, at a mass wedding, I arrive late
as the brides ride on the backs of their grooms,
disappearing into the black waters,
the moon and stars reflecting on the surface,
the marriage certificates spread like confetti
from the backs of convertibles driven by deer
attracted by the promise of high pay
who repeat the prophecies of the past, laughing
at the sight of humans caught in the headlights.

Blue Bodies Litter the Beach

      I stop my wife
as she is about to pick up the first jellyfish,
so blue and small it looks like a shell:
a dark mollusk or tiny anchor
from a long ago wreck
the sea has thrown up.

      A translucent mass tinted pink, blue, & purple,
beckoning even in death's disguise:
like drowned dirigibles,
or an organ removed
from the body of the sky
without muscle or bones,
blood red tentacles trailing behind.

      I do not know
what that inner atmosphere is like,
or if I could breathe the air within;
would it smell as sweet
as the serpent's kiss,
or taste like the ocean bottom:
sand and salt and sunken skeletons.

      Could I look up and launch
the pink ridge of sail,
would I see stars
or stones of tropical reefs,
the shark's tooth's glint
or the sun's glare?
Could I spare the sharp sting
of venom on my wife's skin –
would I beach myself,
would I dream of ships
with sails falling off the edge of the earth?

Part III – Let's Burn the Bed

Let's Burn the Bed

Mikial takes the saw & axe
from the garage
& heads into the small stand
of trees just beyond
the back door,
returning with an armful
of wood: thick logs & kindling
as his wife holds open
the door & says:

"We don't have a fireplace,
Mikial. What have you done?"
"I've brought you a book,"
he says, "before paper,
before paragraph
or sentence, or word."

She takes the wood
from his arms
& carries it into the bedroom
placing it on the duvet
that covers the quilt
into which is woven
the history of suburbia:
a tapestry of strip malls,
taverns, & fast food joints.

"Let's burn the bed,"
she says, "here in this place
of dreams & death
love & sex
breath & the beating
of both hearts:
before thought,
before the birth of born."

Later, Mikial brushes twigs & leaves
from her hair, then caresses the flesh
deep inside the curve of her inner thigh,
as they place their lips together,
tongues & fingers entwined,
launching their voices
before sound or speech
before ink or stone
reciting a catalog of skin & touch,
before language or alphabet
before the naming of words.

She Never Said Goodbye

My friend wrote poetry,
taping her poems
to the wall
and refrigerator door.

She once told me,
"If I wanted to go to heaven
I'd send God a note saying:
Wish you were here."

Claiming she had no religion,
nor wanting to be reborn,
she only asked to be released
and kept one suitcase packed,

joking about carrying
her baggage
wherever she went.

One day, she was gone
and on the table
a napkin and coffee cup
smeared with red lipstick
next to a postcard:
"He's dead.
Mom said to come home."

In the drawer, a broken
heart, still bleeding.

Needles and Ink, Feathers and Wax

You might say
love & sex
are simply a matter of survival.

I say you are a bit
too eager.

Daylight covers me with doubt
& the cold surface
of my own voice
reflects off the walls

like a mirror
polished down
to its back under
    coating.

Still, I hear you call,
waving your arms
like twin branches
all night
tapping on my window.

I fear your touch,
the bright red wound
of your mouth & sex.

Will you stick to me
like a tattoo?

Shall I break out
my needles and ink,
my feathers and wax?

To Tremble, Then Awake

My love, these fires
burn day and night

how deep the moat
that surrounds

your heart, the arrow
that pierces the wind

the gatekeeper
turns the lock

the door swings open
to the unrepentant sky

as I tremble, then awake
to the memory of your flight.

The Cut Above the Heart

The girl in the room upstairs
has the best view,
she says, overlooking
the joggers' path
and tennis courts, cracked
and overgrown with weeds.

The one time she invited
me in for a drink,
we sat on the fire escape
smoking and finishing
off a bottle of wine;
I stayed for breakfast
but she never asked me up again.

After the eggs and toast
and coffee, after the last touch,
when she opened her shirt
to show me the scar
just above her right nipple,
she shoved me out the door,
saying, "that's what you get
when you touch
the third rail of love."

Sometimes at night
I could hear her crying
or making love,
and in the morning
it was always the same,
the door slamming and foot
steps on the stairs heading
down to the lobby alone,
another cut above the heart.

Pretending

I found a house
by the seashore
where the light
filled the windows
with the smell
of the ocean

and in the kitchen
the woman I loved
stood cleaning fish
cutting off the heads
in one smooth blow

while I sliced onions
my tears salting the bread,
"crying won't help," she said
placing the fish
in hot oil and turning
them once, "the skin
falls off," she said,
"if the temperature
is just right."

I squeezed a lemon
the flesh of the fish
flaking off, tasting
of sunlight.

Tomorrow the sun
will rise again,
and it will be her
turn to cry
while I cook breakfast
at just the right temperature
pretending to understand.

The Disappearance

I searched the newspapers
and online for some word
of you or your sudden
disappearance,
contacted your family
and friends, knocked
on strangers' doors
posted signs in shop windows
and on telephone poles,
called the television stations
and radio talk shows
but no one knew
what happened or why,
until I saw the teeth marks
you left along my body
like a fresh tattoo
that appeared overnight
with no explanation
no trace of drugs or alcohol,
only a persistent gnawing
in my chest as if you had sewn
yourself alive, inside.

The Cartographer

*If I needed a name for yesterday,
I would call it the last exit
on Alligator Alley.*

Iron tinged clouds hang
heavy on the horizon –
behind me, saw grass and reptiles

lurk on the banks of the canals
while overhead, turkey vultures
make circles in my rearview mirror.

I told you a story
about my childhood
but made the whole thing up;

you played with the radio
then fell asleep, your head
resting on the window

fogging up the glass;
the road ahead unfurling
into some blank landscape

I filled with the sound
of your breathing,
car chases, and a clutch

of stars I draw against
the darkening sky, connecting
the dots and calling

the constellations after the names
we made up for ourselves:
points of interest on a stolen map.

Confessions of a Sex Fiend

for Miranda

I haven't read a book since Kindergarten
except for *Felix the Cat and His Bag of Tricks*
and the *A & P Home and High School Encyclopedia*
which defines virginity as "an unopened book."

Last winter, I traded love for a used car,
discarding definitions for the etymology
of a blank screen, now so far from home
my GPS speaks with a Dutch accent
and often mistakes toll booths for tulips
    (or is it saying two lips?).

I can no longer tell the difference between
a broken heart or a broken sentence;
and I have no use for therapists in automobiles
though I did once break down
on Alligator Alley somewhere between
Ft. Lauderdale and the National Anthem.

My sister says I am too demanding,
am self-absorbed, cheap, lazy, and rude.
That I love to give advice but not take it,
and date girls who are too thin.

My story, she said, could cure deafness.

I Always Cry at the Movies

As soon as the lights begin to dim,
   my eyes well up.

I sniffle through previews and opening credits;
choke up at each bit of dialogue –
my cheeks wet at every sigh or scream,
stranger or sidekick, savior or serial killer,
sob at beheadings or barbecues
or the slightest hint of a gun,
samurai swords or giant insects,
mistaken identities or cocktail parties.

And when the movie is over,
just before the lights come up,
I look over at you sitting in your seat
as serene as a saint in a French
black and white movie from 1940,
with an angel on each shoulder to guide you,
and I begin to weep
as if it was the end of civilization,
and you and I, assassins of cinema,
could dissolve away into the crowd.

Raising Pigeons

My uncle trained racing pigeons,
keeping them in a wooden cage
in the backyard of his Point Pleasant home.

Talking to them softly every morning,
his voice sounded like round cooing
that the birds answered back

in their New Jersey accents,
complaining about the food and cold
and having to fly around in the rain.

But my uncle, never got angry
or raised his voice, and never
cried in front of the birds, not even

when his wife died of cancer and he took
her body to the cemetery, telling me
in a whisper she would find her way home.

In the Back Yard of the Old House I Found a Rotary Phone

"Pope Rips Mafia; Mob Responds with Dead Lamb"
            - newspaper headline, 1994

quite unexpectedly
the phone rang -

in the hum of the garden
it did not seem
out of place;

flowers stood about
at the end of their wits,
and sunlight

dappled through the tops
and branches of trees;

the blue green grass,
measured by insects & spiders,
tiny gods in aero planes,

butterflies & dragon flies,
approached my waiting ear,
as I answered in my own voice:

"she told me she was no angel -

I never saw any wings;
I searched her body
inside & out;

call me back
when you find the pope's teeth
when you feel the lamb's kiss."

Draw Me!

In an old wooden box I found
in the attic, under the Indian
head pennies and ticket stubs,
I saw a matchbook with the sketch
of a woman's head and Draw Me!
across the front.

All the matches were gone,
but inside I saw a pencil
drawing I had made:
three quick slashes
for eyes and mouth
inside a lopsided oval
with two tiny dots for a nose.

And in my mind, I heard
a voice from the past –
my father's bark:
*Hey Picasso, get out here
and help me tune up the car.*

That old Mustang is long gone,
and my father, too,
nothing left but memories and years
of dust on whatever I collected
from the old house,
like that wooden box,
and on the back of the matchbook
a single black thumbprint
too big to have been my own.

Calligraphy

In the morning,
I lean over
& touch her hair;

so black
& delicately coarse;
woven from rice paddies

& snow-covered streams
that unfold like a brush
painting: dark & bold;

raw silk –
this caravan
from which I will not return.

This Autumn Day

The sky this morning
is gray like an old
cup of tea
with swirls
of oily milk.

I wanted to wander
outside for breakfast;
birds scavenging
for bits of bread
and fat worms waiting
for the rain
warned me away,

I'd rather look up
at the shadow
of the moon
and touch your hair:
color of night,
bend of air.

This Winter Day
(noon)

The clouds are piled up
like a train wreck
across the sky,
and tongues of rain freeze
before they hit the ground.

Back inside the house,
you stir the soup
and spoon out rice
into the celadon bowls.

I see you look up
as I come in the door.

You told me once
the word for snow
in Korean is the same
as the word for eye.

Outside the world
is turning white;
I imagine being lost
in a blizzard

with only the memory
of your glance
to guide me home.

Part IV – Like Black Rocks

The Arboriculturist

Wanting shade
I made a tree:

first, an old step
ladder, wooden
with one missing slat.

For leaves, I took
pages of books
I found discarded
next to the washing machine.

Pictures from magazines
stood for blossoms;
a torn photograph
I forgot to burn
hung like ripened fruit.

But what shall I use
for roots to anchor
my surrogate sapling
this artifice of bark,
sap, and heartwood?

Like Black Rocks

I've created a string
of dark objects
against this white paper:
flat black rocks ringing
the outer edge of the card,
a border that moves
in on itself
meeting in midair.

It is possible
that there is no meaning
here in any language
and there never was.

Only the weight
of emotions
to be placed
in the poet's pocket
before entering
the deepest part
of the lake.

Black and White Cows in the Rain

Last night, I woke to the sound of rain
reminding me of when I was a child
counting the beats between claps
of thunder and slashes of light,
and watching the little dips
and valleys fill up with rain
on the road in front of our house,
just before breakfast on a summer day,
then skipping through the puddles
trying not to step on the reflection
of clouds on the surface of the water,
later watching the cows
after the rain stopped
just before they floated above the earth
like black and white dirigibles,
wishing that I too could fly
into the freshly washed sky.

A Black and Red Ribbon

When I woke up this morning,
my feet walked around the house
by themselves, the rest of my body
only along for the ride.

Outside, I saw blue jays circling
the backyard, carrying parts
of a sentence in their beaks,
the smallest one with only
random punctuation, a seed
        I thought.

Back in the house, I imagined
a typewriter next to the bed,
a black and red ribbon
trailing out the door,
another obsolete opinion
like postcards and letters to the dead.

Writing down your name,
I used words I could not pronounce,
then blindfolded myself
against the approaching avalanche
of acoustic accusations,
my imagination painting over
the blank spaces in the night
unscrewing the moon from the sky.

I Loved Those Jersey Girls

They used to get drunk
and fight over me;
giving me long, hard looks like:
I know you, buddy;
you're just like the other guys,
only worse;
plus, you've got a foul mouth.

But I knew how to soften them up:
sitting and writing poems
in my underwear.
When they woke up,
I'd tell them how good they looked
then read a poem
I wrote the night before.

Just like that, they'd give it up,
sleepy-like and slow
in one long wet embrace
as I leaked metaphors
like an explosion
of jealous juices
behind closed lips.

Forgotten Stops

Riding the subway
late night
too young and dumb
to be scared

sleeping drunks
and forgotten stops
along the way
like missing teeth
on a comb

I lean my head
on the girl's shoulder
she smells of wine
and paradise
her hair tickles my words

I'm writing a poem
in my head
she'll never see
by the time we reach
the last stop
I'll have forgotten her name.

The Short Story

Buried in a box of old journals and notebooks,
I found a short story an ex-girlfriend had written,
documenting a night of hot sex and long, steamy looks
in graphic detail: every earlobe, thigh, & nipple bitten.

"He grabbed me & kissed me hard," the story begins,
but my character goes quickly downhill from there.
"He wasn't in touch with his feelings," she complains,
"until I walked out the door and told him I didn't care."

The story tailspins into a long tearful goodbye,
ending with her barefoot & weeping all the way home,
while I write poison postcards to stick in her fiancé's eye–
but she left behind more than a toothbrush and comb.

Maybe I loved her too much without enough sense;
Even then we knew our story would be written in past tense.

My Friend Writes Poetry When She Can't Sleep

My friend writes poetry when she can't sleep
suffering from insomnia even as a child,
she writes poems on her pillows and sheets.

Biding her time trying hard not to weep,
acting out her fantasies, no matter how wild,
my friend writes poetry when she can't sleep.

With pad and pen into the night so deep,
no matter what the weather, cold or mild,
she writes poems on her pillows and sheets.

Crying over lines she forgot to keep,
she tries rhyme, haiku, any verse style;
my friend writes poetry when she can't sleep.

Picking up men in a library sweep,
searching in every bookstore aisle,
she writes poems on her pillows and sheets.

Trading poems for sex, her clothes in a heap,
words wash ashore like a deserted isle;
my friend writes poetry when she can't sleep;
she writes poems on her pillows and sheets.

Early This Morning

Early this morning
I looked outside my window
and saw my friend, the poet,
emerge from the fog,
droplets of moisture
clinging to his face
like lost words
from an unwritten poem;
with his white hair and beard
he looked like Walt Whitman
wandering into the wrong century;
he stood for a while
and stared at my house
while I waited with my hand
poised on the front door,
but he turned away
and disappeared back
into the fog,
the shape of him
like a cloud drifting
into the morning's news
trailing some fragment
of what he meant
to leave behind.

Queen of the Wasps

My friend, the poet, sifts
through his papers and notes,
then wanders into the backyard
gently poking the earth,
careful so as not to disturb
the Queen of the Wasps.

He brings her a poem
rolled into a tight scroll
as small as a bird's tooth.
"Here," he says, "a song
for your long sleep."
Then returns indoors
calling for his wife,
before he remembers
she is gone.

The Poet Barters for Words

I saw my old friend
walking down the street
pulling a small rowboat
behind him, miles
from any river or lake.

It must be a metaphor,
I thought; the animals
gathering in pairs
at the Barnes and Noble
parking lot, and my friend
who didn't know
how to swim,
feeding the birds
and elephants
while the dolphins
drove up in their
SUVs reciting
sonnets in their
high pitched voices,
books taking the place
of water, rain
the price of a poem.

Collecting Jellyfish

My old friend,
spends his days
hanging out at the beach,
collecting jellyfish
in an empty jar
then taking them
home to his wife.

He spends his evenings
mourning in the garden,
pulling off his clothes,
then plucking the stars
from the night sky
to place on each salty clump
of earth, covering the small
fragile bodies from the sea.

My friend's wife says
she understands him,
dressing in costumes
she made herself,
tattered jeans and tie-dyed
boas made from seaweed
and broken shells,
secretly writing poems
she leaves on her husband's desk
for him to discover each morning.

He takes them down to the beach,
floating them on the waves,
catching sometimes
on the trailing tendrils
of Portuguese men of war –
gifts for drowned sailors
    and old men.

This Is My Ghost Shirt

This is my ghost shirt –
I have hammered it out of paper
& palm fronds;
I have covered it front & back
with paint & dried berries
even the birds refuse to eat:

here I have drawn stick figures,
long extinct mammals,
rain clouds, warriors,
& women w/ exaggerated breasts;

on the back, I scrawl pictographs
& symbols: a snake stands for a river;
a river stands for a snake.

I don't know if the ghost shirt
will make me invisible or invincible,
but I am fairly sure I am impervious
to arrows in 21st century America
though bullets may graze my dancing
figure as I trace circles around the library;

though who will protect me from the tyranny
of language, the words piled up in an empty field
then set fire while I struggle against syllables
& dictionaries, spitting out made-up words
as if they were rain & I could disappear.

Collage

I begin by cutting headlines from magazines
then paste whole sentences
      torn from books;
paragraphs from a Russian novel
or forgotten French short story;
rearranging and editing every line.

The notion of drama appeals to me;
abandoning words
I throw the alphabet into the sea:
where the waves become choked
with alternate endings.

Next, I turn to pictures,
photographs from advertisements,
back issues of magazines,
and newspapers; preferring
inanimate products
to portraits of film stars & politicians.

Tiring of rampant consumerism
& the cult of personality
I switch to landscapes & architectural drawings
coveting the blank face
of winter scenes & concrete bunkers.

Later, I abandon photo realism
& draw primitive figures
with swollen breasts & giant phalluses
on the side of mountains,
ignoring geometry & rules of perspective
opting for short lines & upholstered layers:
an abbreviation or synthesis
like a small jolt of memory, color,
& unformed flirtatious syllables
lodged in the back of the throat.

The House is Full

Unable to sleep one night,
I try counting sheep, automobiles,
and threads in the carpet;
I hear my wife's gentle breathing,
wondering why she remains
indifferent to my insomnia.

Tiptoeing down the stairs,
I see myself at different ages,
spaced out about 10 years apart,
sitting squeezed together on the couch
shoulder to shoulder, knee to knee,
surrounded by words: whole sentences
and paragraphs terrorizing my past selves,
so I push through and amputate
language, torture thought,
& assassinate the dictionary in charge,
rounding up the shivering shades
& shadows, then spitting them out
in the back of an old journal
where they grasp these words
like debris from a shipwreck
when all the lifeboats have gone.

The Restaurant of Books

With a wave of my hand,
I invite passersby into my restaurant:

"Here," I say, "have a seat at this table
next to the window. Compose a sonnet
or a short essay in praise of the view."

First, I offer a salad of *haiku* or *tanka*
& a glass of quotations
from a vintage year;

followed by a meal carefully balanced
with a memoir or novel, contemporary
American or perhaps a 19th century
French *roman a clef* in a new translation.

Dessert is always a thin volume of poems
with a cup of Chinese calligraphy
& for those desiring a *digestif,*
a philosophic essay on epicurean excess
or ancient bookbinding may suffice.
"Thank you for coming," I whisper
as they leave. Then watch them stumble
out into the night with full stomachs
& a parting word chosen at random
from a dictionary or encyclopedia of verse.

www.ingramcontent.com/pod-product-compliance
Lightning Source LLC
Chambersburg PA
CBHW051706040426
42446CB00008B/750